Collins

Spelling

Ages 7–9

quick quizzes

are our fare their fair they're

Jill Atkins

ou or o sounding 'u'

Write the ou or o word that finishes
each sentence.

Each sentence contains a clue to the correct word.

1. My mum's son is my _Brother_.

2. In the hive, the bees make _Hu nee_. x Honey

3. The opposite of old is _Yun___. x ~~~~~~~~~~~~~ x young

4. The five senses are sight, hearing, smell, taste and _Touch_.

5. Friday is a day of the week and September is a _month_ of the year.

6. Dad made a cake and cooked it in the _oven_.

7. If you don't have _enough_ to eat, you will be very hungry.

8. The opposite of below is _above_.

9. The first day after the weekend is _monday_.

10. When I do something wrong, I will be in _trouble_.

11. Another word for twelve is a _Dozen_

12. If my hands are cold, I put on _Gloves_.

13. Europe is a continent, but France is a _country_.

14. The opposite of smooth is _Rough_.

Colour your score

2

Prefixes: mis- and dis-

Write the correct prefix, **mis** or **dis**,
for each word.

1. _mis_ behave

2. _dis_ appoint

3. _dis_ obey

4. _mis_ lead

5. _dis_ appear

6. _dis_ agree

7. _mis_ spell

8. _mis_ judge

9. _dis_ like

10. _mis_ treat

11. _dis_ honest

12. _mis_ match

13. _dis_ own

14. _dis_ qualify

15. _dis_ connect

Read the words
out loud to help find
the correct prefix.

Colour
your score

Prefixes: in-, im- or il-

Tick the word with the correct prefix.

1	inpossible	☐	impossible	☐
2	imdeed	☐	indeed	☐
3	imprison	☐	inprison	☐
4	ilplant	☐	implant	☐
5	improve	☐	inprove	☐
6	inlegal	☐	illegal	☐
7	illiterate	☐	inliterate	☐
8	impulse	☐	inpulse	☐
9	inport	☐	import	☐
10	imdoors	☐	indoors	☐
11	imlogical	☐	illogical	☐
12	incorrect	☐	imcorrect	☐
13	inpolite	☐	impolite	☐
14	infect	☐	imfect	☐
15	immature	☐	inmature	☐

Remember, most words beginning p have the prefix im.

Colour your score

Nouns ending –ation

Remove the suffix **ation** from each noun and turn the root word into a verb.

1. information   to _____

2. occupation   to _____

3. migration   to _____

4. limitation   to _____

5. exclamation   to _____

6. exploration   to _____

7. explanation   to _____

8. declaration   to _____

9. accusation   to _____

10. adoration   to _____

11. sensation   to _____

12. preparation   to _____

13. admiration   to _____

14. imagination   to _____

15. separation   to _____

You may need to change the spelling of the root word.

Colour your score

15 14 13 12 11 10 9 8 7 6 5 4 3 2 1

Suffixes: -ly

Add ly to make each adjective into an adverb.

1 sad _____

2 cheerful _____

3 prompt _____

4 safe _____

5 final _____

6 beautiful _____

7 rapid _____

8 usual _____

9 perfect _____

10 even _____

11 sharp _____

12 slow _____

13 nervous _____

14 quiet _____

15 quick _____

You don't need to change the root word for these examples.

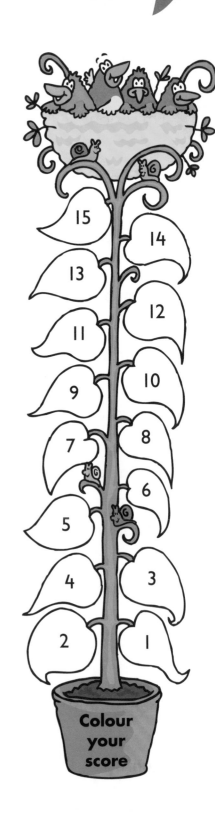

Colour your score

Making adverbs

Add **ly** to change each adjective into an adverb.

Change y to i.

1 happy _____

2 angry _____

3 speedy _____

4 crazy _____

5 lucky _____

6 easy _____

7 busy _____

8 lazy _____

Remove the e.

9 gentle _____

10 humble _____

11 simple _____

Add al.

12 comic _____

13 frantic _____

14 dramatic _____

15 basic _____

The root word spelling needs to be changed before adding ly.

Colour your score

...ing 'k'

...ch each definition.

orchestra	chemist	chorus
...e orchid	stomach	architect
...cter	mechanic	technology
chemistry	school	

Read each clue carefully.

1 A group of people playing music _____

2 A flower _____

3 Where children go to learn _____

4 A person who designs buildings _____

5 A shop where you can get medicine _____

6 A person who can fix your car _____

7 A sound that repeats _____

8 A kind of pain _____

9 This chains a ship to the seabed _____

10 The science of materials _____

11 A person in a story _____

12 Repeated words in a song or poem _____

13 Where our food is digested _____

14 Computers are an example of this _____

15 A plan or plot _____

15
14
13
12
11
10
9
8
7
6
5
4
3
2
1

Colour your score

ch sounding 'sh'

Underline the word in each pair where the **ch** sounds like **'sh'**.

1 brochure   brooch

2 children   champagne

3 chocolate   chandelier

4 chauffeur   chosen

5 chef   chief

6 match   machine

7 moustache   chipmunk

8 parchment   parachute

9 chalet   cherries

10 cheetah   chateau

11 chivalry   chicken

12 squelch   quiche

13 creche   crutch

14 channel   chute

Many words where **ch** sounds like **'sh'** come from French.

Colour your score

-que and -gue

Draw a line to join each word with the right description.

The que words sound like k and the gue words sound like g.

Words ending with que:

1 antique   very ugly

2 unique   lovely – like a picture

3 boutique   something very old

4 mosque   a small shop selling dresses or jewellery

5 cheque   the only one of its kind

6 grotesque   a way of paying for things

7 picturesque   a place where Muslims pray

Words ending with gue:

8 league   a book of things to buy

9 tongue   a serious disease that kills many people

10 rogue   a group of people or teams

11 synagogue   a conversation

12 catalogue   we use it for licking and tasting

13 plague   a speech made by one person

14 dialogue   a dishonest person

15 monologue   a place where Jews pray

Colour your score

Homophones 1

Use the correct **homophone** to complete each sentence.

great or **grate?**

1. "It's really _____ to see you!" I said.

2. The fire was blazing in the _____.

3. I helped to _____ the cheese.

4. I live in a _____ big house.

5. He was a _____ leader of his people.

groan or **grown?**

6. The injured man began to _____.

7. My sunflower has _____ taller than the fence.

8. When I'm _____ up I'll be a scientist.

9. I heard the ship creak and _____ in the stormy sea.

10. These potatoes are home-_____.

fair or **fare?**

11. I paid my _____ when I rode on the bus.

12. The little girl has long _____ hair.

13. I went on ten rides at the _____.

14. "_____ well!" said the alien, as the flying saucer lifted off.

15. It's not _____!

Homophones sound the same, but have different meanings.

Colour your score

15 14 13 12 11 10 9 8 7 6 5 4 3 2 1

11

Spellings to learn

Read, remember, cover and write these words.

1 bicycle	
2 enough	
3 answer	
4 centre	
5 circle	
6 certain	
7 island	
8 address	
9 experiment	
10 favourite	
11 February	
12 believe	
13 quarter	
14 separate	
15 promise	

The more you practise spellings, the easier they will become.

Colour your score

12

-sure or -ture

Add **sure** or **ture** to complete the words in these sentences.

Listen for the slight difference in sound between sure and ture.

1 We did our exercises at the

lei_____ centre.

2 The cows were out in the pas_____.

3 The pirates found the trea_____ in an old chest.

4 The children had an adven_____ in the forest.

5 Who can mea_____ the length of the classroom?

6 I painted a pic_____ of the harbour.

7 The class was learning about na_____.

8 The artist made a sculp_____ of a horse.

9 My grandad likes ma_____ cheese.

10 The sheep were kept in an enclo_____.

11 The men carried the furni_____ into the house.

12 The mountaineer was suffering

from expo_____.

13 I wish I could see into the fu_____.

14 It was a plea_____ to meet you.

15 A weird crea_____ crawled out of the box.

Colour your score

Possessive apostrophes

Put the apostrophe in the correct place for these singular and plural nouns.

	singular	plural
1	a childs toy	the childrens toys
2	a dogs bone	the dogs bones
3	a babys rattle	the babies rattles
4	a lions mane	the lions manes
5	a mans coat	the mens coats
6	a hamsters cage	the hamsters cage
7	an aliens rocket	the aliens rocket
8	a persons name	the peoples names
9	a girls scooter	the girls scooters
10	a boys bike	the boys bikes
11	a womans dress	the womens dresses
12	a soldiers medal	the soldiers medals
13	a hens egg	the hens eggs
14	a pigs curly tail	the pigs curly tails
15	a snakes scales	the snakes scales

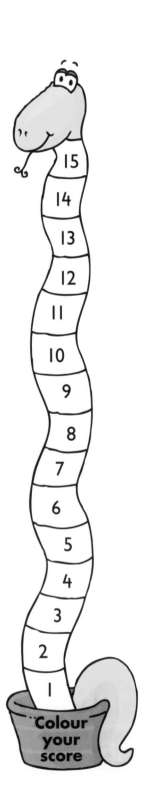

Colour your score

15 14 13 12 11 10 9 8 7 6 5 4 3 2 1

-ous, -eous, -orous or -ious

Circle the correct spelling of each word.

1 poisonous   poisoneous   poisonious

2 sereous   serious   serous

3 ambitious   ambitous   ambiteous

4 dangereous   dangerious   dangerous

5 mountainous   mountaineous   mountainious

6 humorous   humoreous   humorious

7 famious   fameous   famous

8 outrageous   outragious   outragous

9 obvous   obveous   obvious

10 tremendious   tremendous   tremendeous

11 gorgious   gorgeous   gorgous

12 enormous   enormious   enormeous

13 cureous   curous   curious

14 jealeous   jealous   jealious

15 vigorous   vigoreous   vigoruious

If the root word ends in ge, keep the e before ous.

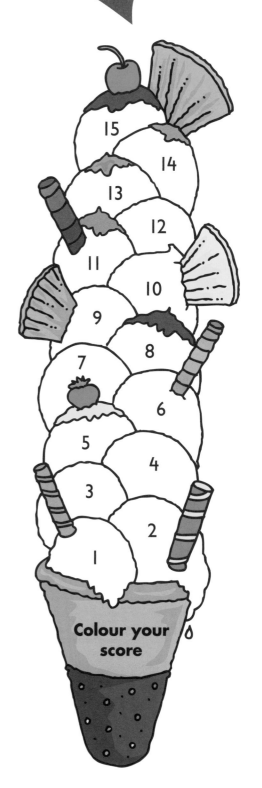

Colour your score

Homophones 2

Write the correct homophone in each sentence.

male or **mail?**

1 Only the _____ lion has a mane.

2 The _____ slipped through the letterbox.

3 I heard a deep _____ voice.

4 The _____ train travelled through the night.

5 My mum sent an e_____ to her friend.

meet or **meat?**

6 Vegetarians don't eat _____.

7 I always _____ my friends at the school gate.

8 My uncle cooked the _____ on the barbecue.

9 My dad loves _____ pie for dinner.

10 What time shall we _____ at the shops?

not or **knot?**

11 I hope it will _____ rain today.

12 There is a _____ in that plank of wood.

13 He tied a tight _____ in the string.

14 I do _____ know what to do.

15 His stomach began to _____ with fright.

Remember, homophones sound the same, but have different spellings and meanings.

Colour your score

15
14
13
12
11
10
9
8
7
6
5
4
3
2
1

16

Important spellings

Write one of these words in each sentence so it makes sense.

imagine difficult perhaps popular
potatoes remember calendar
grammar library history

Practise each word and see if you can spell it on your own.

1 I am learning to use correct __ __ __ __ __ __ __ in my writing.

2 __ __ __ __ __ __ __ is about what happened in the past.

3 My __ __ __ __ __ __ __ __ shows me what the date is.

4 I can borrow books from the __ __ __ __ __ __ __.

5 I helped my grandad dig __ __ __ __ __ __ __ __ from the garden.

6 I try to __ __ __ __ __ __ __ __ how to multiply big numbers.

7 My friend is __ __ __ __ __ __ __ because she is very kind.

8 I can't __ __ __ __ __ __ __ what it would be like to fly like a bird.

9 I'm not sure, but __ __ __ __ __ __ __ I can come.

10 Today, maths was too __ __ __ __ __ __ __ __ __.

10
9
8
7
6
5
4
3
2
1

Colour your score

17

sc or c sounding 's'

Underline the word where the sc or c sounds like 's'.

1. science   scarf
2. chirrup   circus
3. cycle   chrysalis
4. scissors   school
5. criminal   cinema
6. cereal   cherries
7. critical   citizen
8. twice   thick
9. cyclone   crying
10. scenery   screen
11. clearly   celery
12. client   circle
13. pharmacy   practically
14. advocate   advice
15. scent   scheme

sc or c followed by e, i or y make the sound 's'.

Colour your score

Adding suffixes

Add the **suffix** to these words of more than one syllable.

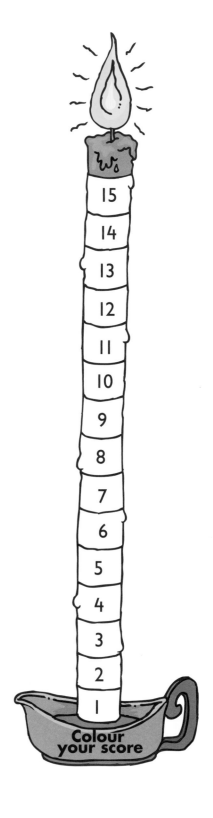

Double the last consonant if that syllable is stressed.

Add ing

1 forget____

2 begin____

3 garden____

4 prefer____

5 target____

Add ed

6 limit____

7 listen____

8 happen____

9 admit____

10 visit____

Add er

11 begin____

12 garden____

13 listen____

14 open____

15 publish____

15
14
13
12
11
10
9
8
7
6
5
4
3
2
1
Colour your score

Suffixes: -sion and -ssion

Draw a line to match each word to its definition.

1 allowed entry — vision

2 the wearing away of soil — division

3 another word for sight — admission

4 sharing — tension

5 tightness or strain — erosion

6 the act of allowing something — collision

7 a crash — invasion

8 payment to retired people — extension

9 an extra part added to a building — permission

10 an attack on a country — pension

11 a special event — expression

12 a choice made — discussion

13 a conversation — procession

14 the look on someone's face — occasion

15 a long line of people walking — decision

> ssion is used if the root word ends in **ss** or **mit**.

Colour your score

20

Different sounds of y

Sort these words into groups by the sound of the letter y.

Egypt	memory	actually	myth
butterfly	cycle	gym	busy	exactly
bypass	chrysalis	myself	deny
pyramid	century		

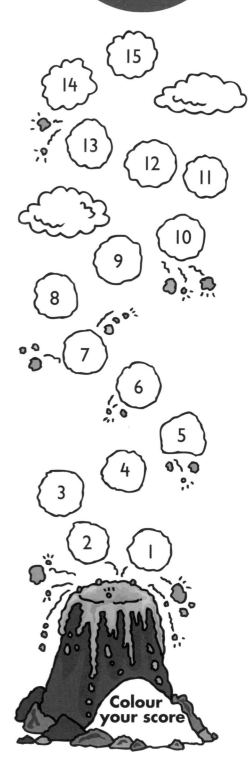

Say each word before you write it.

Colour your score

y sounds like i in it	y sounds like ee	y sounds like eye

ei, eigh and ey words

Choose the correct word to complete each sentence.

Remember, ei, eigh and ey all sound the same.

| weigh   they   eight   neigh   prey |
| sleigh   neighbour   veins   obey   reign |
| reins   reindeer |

1 The plural of he, she or it is _____.

2 Spiders have _____ legs.

3 The queen has had a very long _____.

4 Sam is my next door _____.

5 Santa travels on his _____.

6 I get on the scales to _____ myself.

7 The eagle swooped to catch its _____.

8 The soldier had to _____ orders.

9 The sound a horse makes is _____.

10 Blood pumps along arteries and _____.

11 Rudolph is the red-nosed _____.

12 I pulled on the _____ and the horse stopped.

Colour your score

22

Homophones 3

Write the correct **homophone** in each sentence.

piece or **peace**?

1 I lost a _____ of my jigsaw.

2 Sometimes, I like _____ and quiet.

3 Would you like a _____ of cake?

4 The countries signed a _____ treaty.

main or **mane**?

5 The male lion has a fantastic _____.

6 Our house is on the _____ road.

7 There was a leak in the water _____.

8 We plaited the horse's _____ before the show.

weather or **whether**?

9 I'm not sure _____ I can come or not.

10 In winter, the _____ is cold.

11 I watched the _____ forecast on TV.

12 I wonder _____ it will rain.

Remember, the different spellings have different meanings.

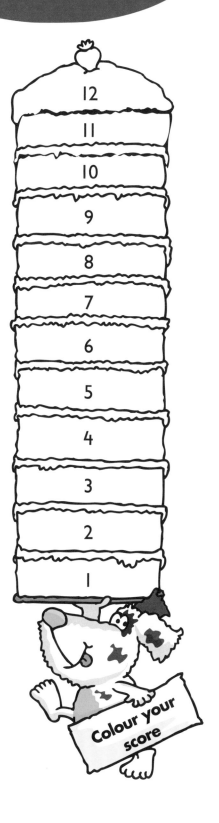

12
11
10
9
8
7
6
5
4
3
2
1

Colour your score

sub-, inter- or auto-

Add **sub**, *inter* or *auto* to the beginning of each word.

1. _____ marine

2. _____ city

3. _____ national

4. _____ heading

5. _____ act

6. _____ tropical

7. _____ biography

8. _____ merge

9. _____ changeable

10. _____ lock

11. _____ graph

12. _____ plot

13. _____ mobile

14. _____ total

15. _____ twine

Sub means under. Inter means among. Auto means self.

Colour your score

24

–tion words

Write the **tion** noun that fits the meaning of each sentence.

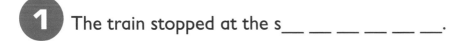

tion is the most common spelling for this sound.

1 The train stopped at the s__ __ __ __ __ __.

2 If you laugh or cry, you show e__ __ __ __ __ __.

3 Story books are called f__ __ __ __ __ __.

4 The wizard mixed a magic drink called a p__ __ __ __ __.

5 Your first year of school is called R__ __ __ __ __ __ __ __.

6 Adding numbers together is called a__ __ __ __ __ __ __.

7 A warning that means "Take care!": C__ __ __ __ __ __.

8 Soldiers stand to at__ __ __ __ __ __ __.

9 Where two roads meet is a j__ __ __ __ __ __ __.

10 If you ask something, it is a q__ __ __ __ __ __ __ __.

11 Part of a whole number is a f__ __ __ __ __ __ __ __.

12 Another word for a country is a n__ __ __ __ __.

13 If you go on holiday, it is your v__ __ __ __ __ __ __.

14 To stop you catching measles you have an in__ __ __ __ __ __ __.

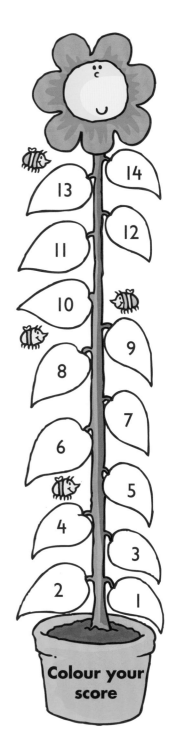

Colour your score

25

Spellings to learn

Draw a line to match each word to its definition.

1 appear   a drug taken as a cure

2 build   construct

3 continue   something you do, or take part in

4 experience   come into sight

5 medicine   carry on

6 ordinary   not long ago

7 position   the rule of a king or queen

8 possession   normal, not special

9 recent   something you own

10 reign   place

11 strange   a set of words that makes sense

12 therefore   in one side and out the other

13 thought   so

14 through   weird

15 sentence   what you think

When you've matched them, try to write the words from memory.

Colour your score

26

Making nouns

Turn these verbs into nouns by adding the suffixes: **ion**, **sion** or **tion**.

verb	noun
1 explode	_____
2 donate	_____
3 elevate	_____
4 object	_____
5 migrate	_____
6 navigate	_____
7 subtract	_____
8 confuse	_____
9 discuss	_____
10 disrupt	_____
11 persuade	_____
12 conclude	_____
13 intend	_____
14 exhibit	_____
15 converse	_____

You may need to change the root word spelling before adding the suffix.

15
14
13
12
11
10
9
8
7
6
5
4
3
2
1

Colour your score

27

Suffixes: –ian

Add **ian** to these words that end with **c**.

1 music_____

2 electric_____

3 optic_____

4 mathematic_____

5 physic_____

6 technic_____

7 magic_____

8 politic_____

Many words ending **cian** are people's jobs or professions.

Choose one of the words above to complete each sentence.

9 A _____ does conjuring tricks.

10 An _____ will mend the light switch.

11 A _____ plays an instrument.

12 A _____ is a member of parliament.

13 An _____ tests your eyes.

14 A _____ is a doctor.

15 A _____ is good with numbers.

Colour your score

Prefixes: anti- and ir-

Add **anti** or **ir** to each word to make
a new word that means the opposite.

**Words beginning
with r use ir.**

1. _____clockwise

2. _____rational

3. _____relevant

4. _____freeze

5. _____social

6. _____responsible

7. _____climax

8. _____replaceable

9. _____regular

10. _____septic

11. _____resistible

12. _____-aircraft

13. _____biotic

14. _____hero

15. _____reparable

Colour
your score

Prefixes: super- or re-

Add **super** or **re** to the beginning of each word.

1 _____market

2 _____try

3 _____appear

4 _____sonic

5 _____turn

6 _____tell

7 _____star

8 _____bug

9 _____fresh

10 _____decorate

11 _____hero

12 _____man

13 _____use

14 _____run

15 _____size

Super means above and re means again or back.

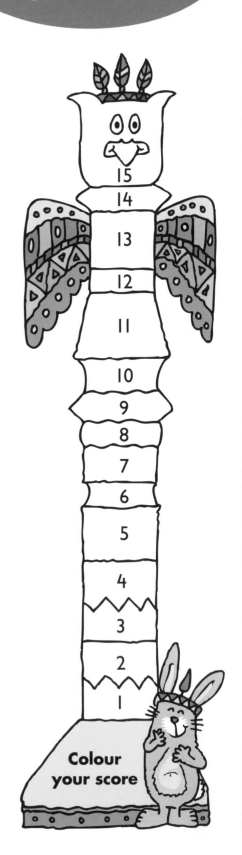

15
14
13
12
11
10
9
8
7
6
5
4
3
2
1

Colour your score

Tricky homophones

Choose the correct **homophone** to complete each sentence.

accept or **except**?

1 Everyone _____ Jim jumped into the pool.

2 Will you _____ this gift from us all?

3 I ate all my dinner _____ the parsnip.

4 I _____ that I need to work harder.

whose or **who's**?

5 I met a boy _____ name is Jack.

6 Guess _____ coming to dinner.

7 This is Anna, _____ my best friend.

8 _____ coat is this?

affect or **effect**?

9 The spell had a strange _____ on the frog.

10 Tiredness can _____ the way you think.

11 The _____ of the tornado was catastrophic!

12 My nerves did not _____ my performance.

Colour your score

12
11
10
9
8
7
6
5
4
3
2
1

Answers

ou or o sounding 'u'
1. brother
2. honey
3. young
4. touch
5. month
6. oven
7. enough
8. above
9. Monday
10. trouble
11. dozen
12. gloves
13. country
14. rough

Prefixes: mis– and dis–
1. misbehave
2. disappoint
3. disobey
4. mislead
5. disappear
6. disagree
7. misspell
8. misjudge
9. dislike
10. mistreat
11. dishonest
12. mismatch
13. disown
14. disqualify
15. disconnect

Prefixes: in–, im– or il–
1. impossible
2. indeed
3. imprison
4. implant
5. improve
6. illegal
7. illiterate
8. impulse
9. import
10. indoors
11. illogical
12. incorrect
13. impolite
14. infect
15. immature

Nouns ending –ation
1. inform
2. occupy
3. migrate
4. limit
5. exclaim
6. explore
7. explain
8. declare
9. accuse
10. adore
11. sense
12. prepare
13. admire
14. imagine
15. separate

Suffixes: –ly
1. sadly
2. cheerfully
3. promptly
4. safely
5. finally
6. beautifully
7. rapidly
8. usually
9. perfectly
10. evenly
11. sharply
12. slowly
13. nervously
14. quietly
15. quickly

Making adverbs
1. happily
2. angrily
3. speedily
4. crazily
5. luckily
6. easily
7. busily
8. lazily
9. gently
10. humbly
11. simply
12. comically
13. frantically
14. dramatically
15. basically

ch sounding 'k'
1. orchestra
2. orchid
3. school
4. architect
5. chemist
6. mechanic
7. echo
8. ache
9. anchor
10. chemistry
11. character
12. chorus
13. stomach
14. technology
15. scheme

ch sounding 'sh'
1. brochure
2. champagne
3. chandelier
4. chauffeur
5. chef
6. machine
7. moustache
8. parachute
9. chalet
10. chateau
11. chivalry
12. quiche
13. creche
14. chute

–que and –gue
1. something very old
2. the only one of its kind
3. a small shop selling dresses or jewellery
4. a place where Muslims pray
5. a way of paying for things
6. very ugly
7. lovely – like a picture
8. a group of people or teams
9. we use it for licking and tasting
10. a dishonest person
11. a place where Jews pray
12. a book of things to buy
13. a serious disease that kills many people
14. a conversation
15. a speech made by one person

Homophones 1
1. great
2. grate
3. grate
4. great
5. great
6. groan
7. grown
8. grown
9. groan
10. grown
11. fare
12. fair
13. fair
14. Farewell
15. fair

Spellings to learn
1. bicycle
2. enough
3. answer
4. centre
5. circle
6. certain
7. island
8. address
9. experiment
10. favourite
11. February
12. believe
13. quarter
14. separate
15. promise

–sure or –ture
1. leisure
2. pasture
3. treasure
4. adventure
5. measure
6. picture
7. nature
8. sculpture
9. mature
10. enclosure
11. furniture
12. exposure
13. future
14. pleasure
15. creature

Possessive apostrophes
1. a child's toy, the children's toys
2. a dog's bone, the dogs' bones
3. a baby's rattle, the babies' rattles
4. a lion's mane, the lions' manes
5. a man's coat, the men's coats
6. a hamster's cage, the hamsters' cage
7. an alien's rocket, the aliens' rocket
8. a person's name, the people's names
9. a girl's scooter, the girls' scooters
10. a boy's bike, the boys' bikes
11. a woman's dress, the women's dresses
12. a soldier's medal, the soldiers' medals
13. a hen's egg, the hens' eggs
14. a pig's curly tail, the pigs' curly tails
15. a snake's scales, the snakes' scales

–ous, –eous, –orous or –ious
1. poisonous
2. serious
3. ambitious
4. dangerous
5. mountainous
6. humorous
7. famous
8. outrageous
9. obvious
10. tremendous
11. gorgeous
12. enormous
13. curious
14. jealous
15. vigorous

Homophones 2
1. male
2. mail
3. male
4. mail
5. email
6. meat
7. meet
8. meat
9. meat
10. meet
11. not
12. knot
13. knot
14. not
15. knot

Important spellings
1. grammar
2. History
3. calendar
4. library
5. potatoes
6. remember
7. popular
8. imagine
9. perhaps
10. difficult

sc or c sounding 's'
1. science
2. circus
3. cycle
4. scissors
5. cinema
6. cereal
7. citizen
8. twice
9. cyclone
10. scenery
11. celery
12. circle
13. pharmacy
14. advice
15. scent

Adding suffixes
1. forgetting
2. beginning
3. gardening
4. preferring
5. targeting
6. limited
7. listened
8. happened
9. admitted
10. visited
11. beginner
12. gardener
13. listener
14. opener
15. publisher